MY BROTHER'S KEEPER?

by the same author

fiction

STAR TURN

MY BROTHER'S KEEPER?

A play by

NIGEL WILLIAMS

faber and faber

LONDON · BOSTON

First published in 1985
by Faber and Faber Limited
3 Queen Square London WC1N 3AU

Photoset by Wilmaset Birkenhead Merseyside
Printed in Great Britain by
Whitstable Litho Whitstable Kent

British Library Cataloguing in Publication Data

Williams, Nigel, 1948–
My brother's keeper.
I. Title
822'.914   PR6073.I432/

ISBN 0–571–13734–2

Library of Congress Cataloging in Publication Data

Williams, Nigel, 1948–
My brother's keeper.
I. Title.
PR6073.I4327M9 1985   822'.914   85–10417
ISBN 0–571–13734–2 (pbk.)

CHARACTERS

MR STONE
MRS STONE
TONY
SAM
TERRY
MR PITTORINI

My Brother's Keeper? was first performed at the Greenwich Theatre, London, in February 1985. The cast was as follows:

MR STONE	Reginald Marsh
MRS STONE	Doreen Andrew
TONY	John McEnery
SAM	John Price
TERRY	Tony O'Callaghan
MR PITTORINI	John Biggerstaff
Director	Alan Dossor
Designer	Dermot Hayes

ACT ONE

*An indication, rather than an elaborate reproduction, of a hospital
ward. Or, rather, one of those neutral rooms that could belong to any
institution. Except, of course, that here there are beds and sick
people. So we may as well assume we are in a hospital. There are no
medical staff in view at the beginning. Only two of the beds are
occupied. One, over to the left of the stage, contains a man of about
60, flat on his back, wired up to bottles and glasses. This is* MR
PITTORINI. *He does not speak and his body seems strapped to the
bed, but his head moves occasionally, from side to side, restless,
pained, like a chained animal. The other occupied bed contains* MR
STONE. MR STONE *is, or was, a classical actor, a man born a little
too late to be as successful as he should have been, and the
extravagance of his gestures and the deep thrill of his voice should be
still perceptible, even though he is paralysed down one side, having
suffered a cerebral stroke. His face too is frozen, and, when he
speaks, he speaks from the side of his mouth. He is staring into space.
Next to him is his* WIFE, *a woman of his age, whose distrait
maternal air conceals a considerable toughness. She is fussing round
his personal effects, on the bedside table.*

MRS STONE: And I'll be back at nine.
  (*He doesn't answer.*)
  OK?
  (*Still no answer.*)
  I have to go home to eat, Alec. I have to eat.
  (*Still no answer.*)
  You're sulking. Don't sulk at me. I have to go home. To
  eat.
MR STONE: When did you say you would be back?
MRS STONE: I said. I'll be back at nine. I said.
  (*Enter from left,* TERRY, *a male nurse. Irish, early thirties.*)
TERRY: Off then, Mrs S?
MRS STONE: He still won't talk to me, Terry.
TERRY: Won't talk? Won't talk? Put your dukes up, Mr S.

9

Let's have your dukes up there?

(*Shadow boxing round him.* MR STONE *does not respond.*)

MRS STONE: It's days. He won't talk. He won't eat. He won't try. Why won't he try, Terry?

TERRY: OK there, Mr Pittorini?

MRS STONE: He seems better today.

TERRY: Yes?

MRS STONE: He seems –

(*But* TERRY *is fussing round* MR PITTORINI.)

I'll be back at nine.

(*Enter* TONY, *the Stones' younger son. He is in his early thirties, dressed with a casualness that is no longer quite so studied as it was. A quick, observant person with a social manner designed to insulate him from the frightening gusts of passion natural to his character.*)

Oh.

(*Pause.*)

Oh.

TONY: Hullo there.

TERRY: Put up your dukes, Mr Pittorini!

TONY: Hi!

(*Pause.*)

Hullo, Dad.

MR STONE: Hullo there.

(*He turns to his wife.*)

MR STONE: You go.

MRS STONE: I'll stay a bit.

MR STONE: You go.

MRS STONE: I don't want to now. I'll stay.

TONY: Look –

MRS STONE: He's cross because I said I had to go.

(*Pause.*)

TONY: Do you?

MRS STONE: I have to eat.

TONY: Right. We've all got to eat.

MR STONE: Get a chair, boy.

MRS STONE: I'll stay a bit.

TONY: Don't let me –

MRS STONE: No no no. That's fine.

TONY: Shall I go, chaps? (*To his* FATHER) Perhaps you'd like to go?

(MR STONE *grins lopsidedly*.)

MR STONE: Yes.

TONY: Yes. Well, I should think you would.

MRS STONE: I'll stay a little while and then –

MR STONE: Then what?

MRS STONE: I thought we might go together. Me and Tony. (*Pause.*) I haven't seen him.

MR STONE: I haven't seen him either.

TONY: Who's seen him? Anyone seen him? (*Turns to* TERRY *who is over by the far beds, the other side of* MR PITTORINI) You seen him?

TERRY: I haven't seen him.

TONY: What's he got –

TERRY: Like what your father had.

TONY: Oh.

TERRY: Stroke.

TONY: Ah.

TERRY: Put your dukes up, Mr Pittorini!

TONY: Will he be – ?

TERRY: He'll be grand. Won't you, Mr Pittorini?

MRS STONE: He's marvellous with them actually.

TONY: Mum –

MRS STONE: He really is marvellous with them. And he's a nurse in fact. A man but a nurse.

TONY: Look –

TERRY: (*On his way out*) Have a care now, Mr Stone! Dukes up, Mr Stone!

MRS STONE: Isn't it incredible?

TONY: I wish you wouldn't talk about people in front of their faces.

MRS STONE: Better than talking about them behind their backs.

TONY: What's that supposed to mean?

MRS STONE: Or writing things about them for that matter.

TONY: Mum, I'm sorry I haven't been. I came when you called. If what you said is happening I'll try to do something about it. I'll –

MRS STONE: Not in front of him, Tony –

TONY: And it's not as if Wonderboy has set bloody foot in the place yet, is it? This is a bloody family crisis then I –

MRS STONE: Not in front of him, Tony . . .

TONY: I thought that was my line.

MR STONE: Go (*Pause.*) Go.

(*She gets up. The row might never have happened.*)

MRS STONE: I'll be in the waiting room.

MR STONE: Uh?

MRS STONE: You might need me.

TONY: I might be –

MRS STONE: What?

TONY: Quite a long time.

MRS STONE: Yes. Yes. (*Bustling off*) Well I'm sure you'll find something to talk about.

MR STONE: I'm sure.

MRS STONE: I'll be in the waiting room. If you need me.

(*And she goes.*)

TONY: She wants me to do something, you see.

MR STONE: Uh?

TONY: I'm on an errand for her. She thinks you've reached Red Alert and I'm on an errand for her.

MR STONE: You what?

TONY: She always was a great one for sending us on errands. And now it's 'Talk to him.' You know? 'Talk to him.' But it's like she wants you to deliver her message. It's like one of those errands. When we were kids.

MR STONE: What did she want you to . . .

TONY: I can't remember. I'll just say what I would say. You know? I won't have conversation subjected to military discipline. I just thought you ought to know I was under orders. (*Mock severe*) You've reached a crisis.

MR STONE: Oh. (*He hasn't really been listening.*) I don't understand . . . women. A minute ago she wanted to eat. Now she doesn't want to eat. I don't understand women.

TONY: Me neither.

MR STONE: Either she wants to or she doesn't. If she doesn't want to eat, why does she say she does? And . . . vice . . .

TONY: Versa.

(*Because of his condition* MR STONE *often loses the thread of his thoughts.*)

MR STONE: Exactly. Why?

(*Pause.*)

TONY: Perhaps she doesn't mean what she says.

MR STONE: Maybe.

TONY: I'm coming to the conclusion that nobody means what they say. And the better they express it the less they mean it. (*Getting up from beside the bed*) I mean you can work as hard as you like at saying what you want to say. If you're in my racket. You can work as hard as you like, putting your back into the business of self-expression. And then you look at it. You get the day's work out and look at it and think, 'Well. What a load of old bollocks. I can't have meant *that*.' So you tear it up and put it in the waste-paper basket and you go back over it again, and after about three days you come up with something that, to your great surprise, strikes you as rather interesting. In fact it is the kind of thing someone else might have said. It seems to have nothing to do with you at all. Whatever it is – it certainly isn't what you meant to say in the first place. It's so long ago now anyway that you've forgotten what it was you *wanted* to say in the first place. You'd have been better off eating a pork pie really.

MR STONE: A pork –

TONY: Can you. . . ?

(*Pause.*)

MR STONE: Understand?

TONY: Yes.

MR STONE: I get . . .

TONY: Confused?

MR STONE: No.

TONY: Tired?

MR STONE: No.

TONY: Fed up?

MR STONE: It'll come in a minute.

TONY: I should stop supplying you with words, right? I should

13

stop sticking my speeches into your mouth, yes? And
probably into everyone else's. These days I am of the
opinion that the only decent course of action for a writer is
to remain totally silent. Occasionally people point as you
pass and whisper 'He's a . . .'

MR STONE: '. . . writer.'

TONY: You're catching on. And you never have to go to the
trouble of committing anything to paper. Which will greatly
enhance your reputation. Because once the arseholes out
there can actually read your work, rather than hearing
about it or participating in it in this mystic way that enables
them to think, somehow, that they alone are responsible for
it or understand it. Well, then you're finished. In the face
of this world silence is the only response.

MR STONE: I don't –

TONY: Understand?

MR STONE: No. (*A struggle to get this out.*) Agree. Don't agree.

TONY: Oh, Dad, it's good to see you.

MR STONE: Good to see you.

(TONY *is suddenly near to tears. He snaps out of it.*)

TONY: You look great.

MR STONE: Yes?

TONY: You look better than him anyway.

MR STONE: Yes. (*Pause.*) Pittorini.

TONY: Yes.

MR STONE: Mr Pittorini. (*Pause.*) He was a railway clerk.

TONY: Yes?

MR STONE: Yes.

TONY: I think it'll be a while before he's taking tickets again.

MR STONE: He's –

TONY: On the way out?

MR STONE: He's –

TONY: Italian?

MR STONE: No. He's –

TONY: A dummy. (*Pause.*) Well, you almost laughed.

MR STONE: He's very ill.

TONY: You can say that again.

MR STONE: He's got –

TONY: What?

MR STONE: Same thing as –

TONY: Same thing as you?

MR STONE: Same thing.

　　(TONY *looks at* MR PITTORINI.)

TONY: Blimey. Prognosis doesn't look too good.

MR STONE: Is Sam going to –

TONY: Don't you hear what I've been doing?

MR STONE: What you've been –

TONY: Up to.

　　(*It's very easy to deflect* MR STONE. *He has a puzzled, childlike look. But* TONY *speaks fast.*)

　　Rehearsing another . . . you know . . .

MR STONE: Load of . . .

TONY: Right.

MR STONE: Yes.

TONY: You'll never stop working now.

MR STONE: No?

TONY: Disabled actors are in fashion at the moment. All the rage.

MR STONE: But not . . . real . . . (*Pause.*) People pretend to be . . . whatever . . . OK . . . but the real thing . . . (*A shudder.*) No.

TONY: What's it like?

MR STONE: What?

TONY: The real thing.

MR STONE: This?

TONY: Yes.

MR STONE: Pretty awful.

TONY: Yes. (*Again a sudden attack. Almost tears . . .*) Oh, Dad . . .

MR STONE: What is this . . .

TONY: Play?

MR STONE: Play, yes.

TONY: We're really doing well now. In the last four interchanges I have correctly guessed what it is you were about to say. Problem is – does this simply mean that you are allowing me to influence your choice of remark? I think

15

we need a bit more incomprehension really. To make this dialogue meaningful. A bit more opposition don't you think? (*Watching his* FATHER) I wish you wouldn't watch me with such pride. It makes me want to cry.

MR STONE: That's OK.

TONY: The play's a swinging attack on something or other. I forget what. The National Health Service probably. Or maybe I've gone really deeper this time. It's an attack on illness. I hit illness pretty hard. I expect the critics will have a hard time coming to terms with that. I'm doing my errand, you know. For Her. I'm not coming to the point, am I? I'm –

MR STONE: Is Sam –

TONY: I can remember you in that theatre in Leicester. When Mum took us. Remember? It was a crummy production I expect but when you came out I couldn't believe my luck. That was my dad up there. It was rep actors and all the rest of it but when you came out –

MR STONE: 'Blow winds and crack your cheeks. Spout you –'

TONY: Hurricanoes.

MR STONE: (*He has trouble saying it.*) Hurricanoes. Lovely word. (*Pause.*) I sit here and think about words. I can't quite –

TONY: Get them.

MR STONE: Get them. But they come before me in a sort of . . .

TONY: Procession.

MR STONE: All right.

TONY: Weren't you a bit young to be playing Lear?

MR STONE: I was a bit old to be playing Hamlet.

TONY: In the same season. (*Pause.*) But to me it's never been as real as that night. I didn't know whether Lear was my father or my father was Lear. But the two were hopelessly confused. After that I never had any disbelief to suspend when I was in a theatre. I believed it all.

MR STONE: 'How sharper than a serpent's tooth it is . . .'

TONY: He likes it.

MR STONE: Uh?

TONY: Pittorini. Pittorini likes it. He's a fan.

MR STONE: 'Plate sin with gold and the strong arm of . . .'

16

TONY: Justice, Dad. Justice. (*Going to him*) She wanted me to
say that –
(*As he is about to get around to his errand, from the back comes
SAM, TONY's elder brother. A man of 40. In a suit. A
businessman with an almost brutally buttoned-down manner. At
first sight you might almost call him pompous. Immediately
TONY sees him he freezes. The tension between these two is
almost palpable.*)
Oh.
SAM: Oh.
(*Enter MRS STONE.*)
MRS STONE: I told him to go through. Was that all right?
TONY: Yes. Of course. I –
MRS STONE: I phoned him, Tony. He said he might come
today.
TONY: In case I threw a bedpan at him?
MRS STONE: Tony, I wanted him to –
SAM: Hullo, Dad.
MR STONE: Hullo there.
MRS STONE: Shall I stay then?
SAM: Of course, Mum.
TONY: 'Of course, Mum.'
MR STONE: Get a chair.
SAM: Of course, Dad.
TONY: 'Of course, Dad.'
MR STONE: You go.
MRS STONE: I thought –
MR STONE: Wait outside.
MRS STONE: The Lord and Master. (*But she gets up.*) All right,
love.
SAM: Do you really want to go, Mum?
TONY: She likes to allow him to pretend to be in charge.
MR STONE: You what?
TONY: Nothing, Dad.
SAM: Don't go if you don't want to, Mum.
MRS STONE: I'll be in the other room if you want me.
MR STONE: Yes yes yes yes. Chair.
SAM: Mum –

17

TONY: We're not going to eat you, Samuel. Yet.

MRS STONE: I'll be there.

(*She turns at the door.* SAM *is getting another chair.*)

He came, Tony. He did come.

TONY: I can see.

MRS STONE: All right, then. All right.

(*She goes.*)

TONY: Christ!

SAM: What's up with you?

TONY: I've had a bad day at the office.

SAM: I thought that was my line.

TONY: We're all pinching each other's lines today. Didn't you know?

SAM: Well, I'm here.

TONY: So everybody keeps saying. Are you going to sing?

SAM: Don't let's talk about the stage.

MR STONE: We're on it.

SAM: Sorry?

MR STONE: Hospital. What's a hospital but a –

TONY: Stage.

SAM: I see.

TONY: Make-up have done a fantastic job on him I must say.

SAM: Tasteful as ever, I see.

TONY: You've developed a line in caustic wit since I last saw you, Samuel.

SAM: Perhaps I've flowered in your absence.

TONY: Either that or you're an alien being who has taken over my brother's body. Instead of the usual alien being that took over his body at about the age of 8.

SAM: You haven't changed at all. In fact I think you're still wearing the same jacket. Is it supposed to be working class?

TONY: No. It's supposed to be warm.

SAM: Because it doesn't look working class. It looks shabby but middle class. It's got tomato down the front of it.

TONY: Oh, well, I had a first night last night . . .

SAM: What are those up there?

TONY: Get-well cards. For Mr Pittorini over there.

SAM: Bit late for that isn't it?

TONY: It's never too late for that.
  (MR STONE *has wandered off into a dream.* SAM *is over by* MR PITTORINI's *bed.*)
  GET WELL SOON.
  (SAM *looks down at* MR PITTORINI *who is asleep.*)
  'Soon.' My God. They could have left out the 'soon'. That seems to me to be a totally sadistic piece of black humour. GET WELL SOON. They could have altered it to GET WELL PROBABLY. OR TRY NOT TO HAVE ANOTHER RELAPSE. Or –
MR STONE: Die. They could have said – Die.
TONY: Dad –
  (SAM *goes back to his* FATHER.)
SAM: I'm sorry I didn't come, Dad. There's a reason. I –
MR STONE: OK. That's OK.
SAM: I haven't been . . .
TONY: Well.
MR STONE: Uh?
TONY: What's been the trouble, Sammy?
SAM: My wife left me.
TONY: But that's *great*. That's fantastic. She finally left you. That's amazingly good news.
SAM: (*Angry and irritated*) For God's sake, Tony –
TONY: I mean you won't have to put up with any more of her fucking awful food or her fucking awful hairstyles or her fucking awful friends. No more Toni, no more Denise, no more –
MR STONE: Jacky –
  (*This is not meant maliciously. He simply hasn't quite caught on to what the conversation is about.*)
SAM: SHUT UP THE PAIR OF YOU, WILL YOU?
TONY: Sssh. You'll wake Mr Pittorini. His leg'll fall off.
SAM: Does he understand what we're saying?
TONY: Mr Pittorini? I don't think Mr Pittorini even knows he is Mr Pittorini. He's very ill. And Italian presumably.
SAM: Dad. I mean Dad. Does Dad understand what we're saying?
TONY: Of course. This is your first visit, isn't it? It must be a bit of a shock for you to walk in and see him looking as if

he's just had a long sleep in a fridge. You can get away with murder. If we speak quickly, in French, we can say nasty things about him to his face.

SAM: Dad – did you understand? What I said?

MR STONE: I understand for a little while. And then things become . . . blurred. I watch, you see . . . but I'm a bit . . . outside it. Like watching a play. Like a play. All in a play. (*Looking between them*) Please don't argue, boys. Please don't fight. (*Pause.*) Were you arguing?

TONY: We were just continuing a discussion we began last time we met.

SAM: We haven't seen each other for four years.

TONY: Oh, was that the time I called you a stuck-up –

SAM: We're not going to talk about that.

TONY: Yet.

SAM: I'm sorry I haven't been to see you, Dad. Joan left me.

MR STONE: You said.

SAM: It's been coming. I mean it was going to come. I just – (*Stops himself.*) Anyway. I've got a book. It's about what you've got. It's a sort of handbook. I read it in the train coming up.

TONY: Oh, this is incredible, Sammy. This is incredible.

SAM: Are they giving you physiotherapy?

TONY: Hasn't been near him for four weeks and he's an expert already.

MR STONE: A woman comes round. And pulls at my legs. 'I could be bounded in a nutshell and count myself a king of infinite space,' I tell her. It's a question of the soul, I tell her. But she doesn't want to talk about the soul. She wants to talk about my arms and legs. She doesn't want to hear about my immortal longings.

SAM: If you can walk, you see, Dad –

TONY: Are you reading from her script word for word, Sammy? Did she hand it to you on the way in? I expect she knew I wouldn't deliver the message the way she wanted it. She really is taking serious action, isn't she? (*With hatred and contempt*) He isn't a fucking car battery you know. He's a person. You can't get him started from a handbook.

SAM: Shut up, can't you?

TONY: Yes, I can. I *can*. But . . . (*Suddenly weary*) Perhaps I should go.

MR STONE: Both of you stay. I want you both here . . . to . . .

TONY: Stay.

MR STONE: Yes. Stay.

SAM: I've got some exercises for you.

TONY: Word for word. Jesus, it's for bloody word. Have you two been rehearsing outside?

> (*But* SAM, *getting back into the swing of this war has decided to ignore his* YOUNGER BROTHER. *The quickest way of getting him riled. He sits in front of his* FATHER.)

SAM: Now. Can you lift this?

TONY: I don't think so.

MR STONE: This side. It's –

SAM: Right. Now the left.

MR STONE: This. This is OK.

SAM: And use the left one to lift that and lean . . .

MR STONE: This one?

SAM: That's right. That's *right*.

> (TONY *has got right up behind* SAM.)

TONY: And if you stick out the bum, Samuel . . .

SAM: See what I mean? Lean forward with the right . . .

TONY: And really get the bum back in the chair.

SAM: That's it. Good.

TONY: Good. It's a good bum. It's a vital part of your equipment as an executive is your bum. You spend, after all, most of your working life sitting on it and telling proles what to do. So what has happened to you, Samuel, is serious. You have *lost the use of your bum.*

SAM: Harder. Get your hands round it.

MR STONE: I can't quite . . .

SAM: That's it, Dad.

TONY: You've had a total eclipse of the bum, Samuel. But if you continue with this course of exercises, if you continue to lean patronizingly over your nearly defunct Dad and tell him the ten easy steps he needs to take to get better as per you and Mrs Stone then I think you will find sensation flooding back to your arse once more.

(*And indeed as* SAM *leans forward in his chair his executive behind is somewhat visible.*)

SAM: Up . . .

MR STONE: Hurts.

SAM: Higher. Can you feel that?

TONY: Can you feel that, Samuel?

SAM: Excellent.

TONY: Yes, your behind is about to get up off its arse and –

SAM: SHUT UP, CAN'T YOU? FOR ONE MINUTE! CAN'T YOU LEAVE IT ALONE, YOU LITTLE SQUIRT! (*Turning on him*) Look, it isn't easy to come here after the things that have been said about me in this family. If you want to know – it was pretty bloody difficult. I know what you say about me. You've probably poisoned her mind now as well. If I finally do decide to come maybe it isn't just because she's called me, maybe it's because I think it's time somebody did something to make it up, my God, that we could have got to this point makes me feel . . . Jesus, when I came in I thought, 'Who is that old man?' I –

MR STONE: Come here.

SAM: Daddy –

(SAM *is near to tears.*)

MR STONE: Come here.

(*Awkwardly his* FATHER *puts his arms around him.*)

TONY: Oh, my Gawd. (*To* MR PITTORINI) Sex, Mr Pittorini. Sex between father and son. What do you make of that, Mr Pittorini? (*To them*) I've got an exercise for Mr Pittorini. If he can roll his left eyeball we give him a Smartie. Good idea?

SAM: (*Angry*) Tony!

TONY: (*Mock histrionics*) 'God may forgive you but I never shall.'

MR STONE: Queen Elizabeth.

SAM: And he's God?

TONY: He's our father, Sammy. And if he isn't in heaven he's pretty uncomfortably close to it.

SAM: You accuse me of being callous. You're a callous little sod,

22

you are. Are you jealous? Is that it? Is no one even allowed
   a look in?
TONY: I remember when we used to share a bed you'd never let
   me wank.
SAM: Well, it's disgusting.
TONY: All I wanted to do was to creep off to the other end of
   the bed and have myself away. So off I'd go. Get going.
   And then I'd get this curious little voice in the dark. 'What
   are you doing?' Rustle rustle. 'Nothing.' 'You sure?' 'Sure.'
   Long pause. Then . . . rustle rustle rustle rustle . . .
SAM: Oh, for God's sake, if we're going to go back to who did
   what to whom in the playground then –
TONY: Then what?
SAM: I don't . . . (*Pause.*) I don't remember things like you.
   (*Pause.*) I just get on with it. (*Pause.*) It hurts me too, you
   know.
TONY: Not enough for me, sister.
SAM: Stop pretending to be a queer.
TONY: Who's pretending?
SAM: STOP IT!
   (*Enter* TERRY.)
TERRY: All OK?
SAM: Fine. Fine.
TERRY: You could lose yourself in this hospital.
SAM: Getting a bit –
TONY: Emotional.
TERRY: All right there, Mr Stone?
MR STONE: Fine. Fine.
TERRY: He shouldn't be here really.
TONY: Where should he be? Crufts?
TERRY: This isn't where he should be. Nor Mr Pittorini
   neither.
TONY: I think Mr Pittorini should be on Channel Four actually.
TERRY: No beds.
TONY: I can see nothing but beds.
TERRY: No beds where they should be. In Scutari. They should
   be in Scutari. But Scutari's full to bursting.
TONY: Where's this then? Waterloo? Anzio?

TERRY: It's nothing really. It's not what you'd call a ward. It's a shed really, that's all it is. (*Watching the two of them*) Did your ma ask the two of you down, then?

SAM: That's right.

TERRY: Yes. It's very critical.

SAM: Yes?

TERRY: He won't eat, Mr Stone. He's gone three days. And he won't –

SAM: Try.

TERRY: That's it. That's it exactly. Well. It's very critical, I suppose. (*Pause.*) Perhaps you'll be able to . . . do something.

TONY: That's why we're here.

TERRY: It's a question of the will, you see.

SAM: Yes.

TERRY: The will to live. You know?

TONY: I remember.

TERRY: I think Mrs Stone thought . . .

TONY: That the mere sight of the two of us would send him hobbling off down the ward. Real psychological insight.

TERRY: I think she –

TONY: I think she's playing Happy Families, Terence. But I think it's a bit late for that.

TERRY: I think –

TONY: I think she wants Sammy and me to put on a cabaret act.

TERRY: Mrs Stone –

TONY: Anyway we'll remember that. The will to live. We'll remember that.

TERRY: I'm in Scutari if you need me. Just over there.

TONY: I can see it. The wounded strapped to horses, awash with dysentery. And there's Florence, bending over one of the – (*But* TERRY *has gone.*)

SAM: He's gone. (*Pause.*) And there was no need to be rude to him.

TONY: Patronizing bastard. 'The will to live.' What does he expect us to do? Tell him to snap out of it?

SAM: He's here. He's doing his best. I don't know.

TONY: How do you give someone the will to live?

24

SAM: In an hour.

TONY: Oh, is that all you've got?

SAM: I've got a meeting.

TONY: Oh, a *meeting*. Well, you'll have to get off if it's a *meeting*, won't you? Anyway, someone with your charm and forcefulness didn't really need to come, did you? You could probably give someone the will to live by sending them a memo. Or in extreme cases a bottle of white wine.

SAM: I told you, Tony. I just –

TONY: You just wanted to retreat. The way you always do. The way you did that night. Because you think it'll go away. Well, it won't go away. I'm sorry. But I'm still angry at you. I can't –

SAM: WE'RE NOT GOING TO DISCUSS THAT!

TONY: Yet, Samuel. Yet. (*Elated*) 'Ello 'ello 'ello, he's woken up.

SAM: Well, you talk to him then. If I'm not allowed to do his exercises, you do it your way. You give him the fucking will to live.

TONY: No problem. I revive corpses every day. Christ, the *Times Literary Supplement* said I had 'compassion'.

SAM: Shows how much they know.

TONY: I'm a national hero in Finland.

SAM: Where is Finland exactly?

TONY: I'm huge in Denmark.

SAM: Is it any good being huge in Denmark? Does it help?

TONY: Not really.

(*This banter, the language of their childhood, has almost brought them, briefly, together.*)

SAM: I wish we could . . .

TONY: Maybe we could. If we could . . .

SAM: What?

TONY: Christ, we're getting as bad as him.

SAM: How do you mean?

TONY: You know. Unable to . . .

SAM: Unable to what?

TONY: Finish our . . . things . . . you know.

SAM: Finish our what?

TONY: Sentences. You know. Sentences.

MR STONE: Was I asleep?

TONY: You ran all over the ward. Screaming and shouting.

MR STONE: Did I?

TONY: You were Othello. Briefly.

MR STONE: 'Put up your bright swords or the dew will . . .'

TONY: '. . . rust them.'

MR STONE: There is no longer room for the classical gesture in the English theatre.

TONY: There is no longer room for *your* classical gesture, you mean. You should have had more than one.

MR STONE: The other fellow. Sir . . .

TONY: Sir Thing.

MR STONE: He pinched all the other classical gestures. He got to the shop early and pinched them all. He's a very dull actor is Sir Thing.

TONY: And he's not disabled.

MR STONE: The final proof of his essential dullness. All the best people are disabled. Think of the huge number of parts written for people paralysed down one side. Hundreds of them.

TONY: And if there aren't, then we should make bloody sure that the quota is kept up. We should get right on to the GLC and make pretty damn sure that there are parts being written for people paralysed down one side.

MR STONE: Positive . . .

TONY: Discrimination. Quite. Imaginative casting. All that's required.

MR STONE: Laertes . . .

TONY: Clearly paralysed down one side. If you look at the text closely.

MR STONE: Ophelia –

TONY: Mr Pittorini could play Ophelia. He'd make a good Ophelia.

MR STONE: You could . . .

TONY: Retitle them. Why not? *Half the Prince of Denmark.*
Duke Lear. All's Well That. And not just the classics. The National Theatre of the Paralysed Down One Side presents

26

Quarter of a Sixpence. The –
(*He has run out of steam.*)

SAM: When you breathe life into things, Tony, it's always your life. Not their life. (*Getting up*) They want to feel a bit free. They don't want you telling them they're free.

TONY: Except in Finland.

SAM: (*Big brother, hard, without emotion*) Oh, you always had such life. As a little kid you had such *life* in you. I can remember when you were born. Going to the hospital to see you. I was nearly 10. Christ. Nearly 10. An old man. And there was you like a little red rat. Screaming and punching and just . . . well . . . just *alive*. And you never stopped being alive. You never stopped waddling up to people and looking up into their faces and letting them know how bloody alive you were. (*Pause.*) But it was just you, Tony. It wasn't the other buggers. It was just you. It was just you having this good time. You had this life. And you carried it around like a candle flame and you hoped it would set light to the grass and the trees and the buildings and the streets until all of England was blazing with this light of yours. You called it all sorts of names but *all* it was, in the end, was this life of yours. And it'll set light to nothing, Tony. Not in the big wide world outside not here not even in fucking Finland. Because while you've been carrying this life of yours so carefully in your hands people have been dying and failing and going dark. All round you. Everywhere. (*Pause.*) He is going to die, Tony.

TONY: He isn't.

SAM: He is.

TONY: HE ISN'T!
(MR STONE *snaps awake.*)

MR STONE: Was I asleep?

TONY: I don't know, Dad. I don't know.

MR STONE: I heard voices. I do get tired. (*Looking at the two of them fondly*) Carry on. Carry on. (*Pause.*) I do get tired.

SAM: You like to hear us talk, don't you?

TONY: So long as you can't hear what we're saying.

SAM: Fathers expect their sons to listen.

TONY: You're the expert on fatherhood.

SAM: Listen. Alison –

TONY: We're not going to talk about Alison. Yet. Alison's a distasteful subject. (*Does grotesque gibbering impression:*) ''Ullo, Daddy . . .' (*Pacing*) She should have been exposed at birth. We don't miss her at all. She couldn't even walk straight.

SAM: Tony. I just –

TONY: The death of a child isn't inevitable. That's why it's easy to accept. That's what I believe. The only thing I can't accept is the inevitable.

SAM: Tony – (*Gives up.*) I thought you were supposed to be a Marxist.

TONY: I'm a coffee-table Marxist. I'm an ersatz Marxist. I'm –

SAM: Well, carry on then. Carry on. Since I am not allowed to hold the poor old bastard's arm for him.

TONY: Sam –

SAM: Carry on. Carry on. The stage is yours. Tone.

(*And* TONY *goes to his* FATHER.)

TONY: Dad –

MR STONE: Hullo, boy.

TONY: What do you think about?

MR STONE: When?

TONY: Now.

MR STONE: I think about the old days.

TONY: When?

MR STONE: Before the –

TONY: War.

MR STONE: And afterwards. When you were kids. You know? I think about that a lot.

TONY: And is it like . . . being there?

MR STONE: Yes. Yes, it is.

SAM: Living is what you do now, isn't it? Or what you plan to do tomorrow.

TONY: Living is what *you* forgot to do yesterday.

SAM: You think that talking about things makes them live again. Mentioning them confers some kind of grace upon them. Can't imagine *why*. You can talk all you like. You and he

like to talk. But talk won't change anything. A hospital bed
is a hospital bed is a hospital bed. Except in your precious
bloody theatre, things are what they are, I'm afraid. And
death is just that. Just nothing. You understand?

TONY: Did you come back just to hurt him?

MR STONE: Come here, boy.

(SAM *moves to him*.)

You look . . . tired. What's happening?

SAM: I'm sorry I said the things I said, Dad. It was Joan. All of
that. People in our family are not supposed to make
trouble, you know? Well, I am. I'm supposed to be the
steady one. And . . . (*Pause*.) I don't know. Still at the
factory. Still churning it out. Nobody thanks you for it.
Nobody thanks you for actually *working* in this day and age.
'Ballbearings? Ooh, *funny*!' (*As a challenge*) Somebody's got
to do it.

MR STONE: You're not arty, Samuel. He's arty. I'm arty. But
you're not arty.

SAM: Can't I even try to be?

TONY: Quiz. Quiz. Dad – who said to who and in what
production – 'If you would cry a little less, young lady, I
think the audience might cry a little more'?

MR STONE: I don't approve of crying on stage. Nothing
warrants crying on stage. Except possibly the sighting of
Milton Shulman in the third row from the front. (*Shrewdly*)
I know what you're doing. I know she's said something to
you. But it's no good. You should concentrate on
yourselves not me. I want to see you two . . .

TONY: What?

MR STONE: You know what . . . that thing . . . you know . . .
between people . . .

TONY: Rope?

MR STONE: The thing that . . . grows . . .

TONY: Grass?

SAM: Tony!

MR STONE: Love . . .

TONY: Oh, *love* . . .

MR STONE: Not me. Look. Good acting is a matter of

observation. Not of being. If I can't do it. If I can't do it. Then. Finish. You see? You see? I've made up my mind really. Finish.

SAM: (*Reassuring*) You mustn't say that! You aren't finished. (*Pause.*) Don't listen to him, Father. It isn't just talk. There are things you can do. Practical things. Exercises. Look, it could be worse. You could be stretched out like that thing over there.

TONY: I resent these slurs on Mr Pittorini. Mr Pittorini will be in the Royal fucking Ballet by the time I've finished with him. And he won't need any textbooks neither. He'll be hopping round the ward on a pogo stick. An' you know how he's gonna do it. By the powah of love. Praise the Lord.

SAM: Mother said –

TONY: I know what 'Mother' said, and I told you. Or if I didn't tell you I'm telling you now. I'm not running any errands for that old bat.

SAM: Why do you criticize everything she says?

TONY: Because I don't think she's ever said anything remotely interesting, that's why. I've known her for over thirty years. I think I've heard everything she's ever said. Twice. And I don't think she's ever said anything remotely interesting. I keep thinking she might. I crouch by her open mouth waiting. The suspense is unbearable. But up to now she has managed to avoid ever saying anything that is of any interest at all.

SAM: This is just because of Ella, isn't it?

TONY: It isn't just because of Ella –

SAM: It's Alison and –

TONY: SHUT UP ABOUT ALISON! ALISON DOESN'T EXIST IN THIS RIGHT LITTLE TIGHT LITTLE FAMILY! SHE IS A NON-PERSON, SHE HAS NO LEGAL EXISTENCE FOR MRS STONE, YOU UNDERSTAND?

(SAM *stays silent.*)

SHE NEVER FUCKING CAME, SAM! NONE OF YOU CAME! HE WAS THE ONLY ONE WHO CAME! SHE NEVER EVEN TURNED UP! (*Pause.*) What is it about Ella, I used to ask myself, that

30

inspires such hostility? Why is it that this perfectly innocuous woman, my wife, should inspire such a torrent of loathing? Is it that she hasn't got a trouser suit? Is that where she went wrong? Joan wore a trouser suit. They couldn't get you married to Joan fast enough, could they? It was when you started playing, he started on you.

SAM: I don't know why she doesn't like Ella. I just don't know. But you couldn't leave it alone. You pushed her at them, didn't you? You wanted to prove something.

TONY: Such as?

SAM: That you needn't need Mother.

TONY: I don't.

SAM: You're afraid to.

TONY: I am. And with bloody good reason, may I say. She'd have me for breakfast, would our mother. She bloody had you for breakfast, didn't she?

MR STONE: Don't talk like that.

TONY: *Good* –

MR STONE: Don't talk like that about your mother. I shall –

TONY: Colour returns to cheeks. Patient looking better.

MR STONE: I tell you, boy, I shall –

TONY: Oh yes, Dad. Dad. (*With immense sadness*) I want you to lift your hand to me.

MR STONE: I can't, Tony. It's no good any more.

TONY: Can't you even hit me, you old toad? You used to be good at that.

MR STONE: I can't –

(*He's given up. Almost in tears.*)

SAM: For God's sake, Tony –

MR STONE: Did I hit you?

TONY: Frequently.

MR STONE: I'm sorry.

TONY: Please don't apologize. (*To* SAM) Try the exercises. If I go on like this I'll have finished him off by the time they bring round his tea.

MR STONE: Exercises . . . I don't think . . . tired.

SAM: It's just what she said, Tony. He doesn't want to know. We have to do something. We have to do something.

31

TONY: But what?

SAM: Maybe we should – (*Pause.*) Look, I am sorry. I am sorry I didn't come to the funeral.

TONY: Oh Christ, don't worry about that. It was a really tacky funeral anyway. It got terrible reviews. You aren't peacemaking by any chance are you? Are you labouring under the delusion that if we throw our arms round each other he will leap to his feet and dance round the ward singing 'If I were a rich man' because he won't. Families thrive off hatred and resentment and years of stored-up bitterness.

SAM: I just couldn't –

TONY: Face it. I understand. Funerals are so sort of . . . dead somehow, aren't they? And they're always the fucking same. Always the same *coffin*. I think the design of the British coffin is appallingly unimaginative, don't you? And they always do the same thing with it. Drop it into the ground or shove it into the incinerator. I think funerals should be much more impromptu. Wackier. Don't you?

SAM: Well, I am. I'm sorry.

(*A sign of a crack in the blazing hostility between these two. But, in accord with the rules of this relationship, it is immediately suppressed.*)

TONY: Do you suppose he was an ice-cream man?

SAM: Who?

TONY: Pittorini.

SAM: You're getting obsessed with Pittorini.

TONY: I get a lot of feedback from him.

SAM: Tony –

TONY: A lot of response. I think he may be a potential father figure. If things go like this I may need one.

(PITTORINI *stirs. Thrashes and then falls back, his eyes closed.*)

I wonder what he did.

SAM: When?

TONY: When he wasn't strapped to a bed with his brain in splints. (*Going over to him*) Perhaps he was a restaurateur. 'Pittorini's.' 'Let's all go to Pittorini's.' 'Not Pittorini's

32

again.' Or an acrobat maybe. The Pittorini Brothers. Direct from Milano. This amazing troupe will perform feats that will make your eyes water. (*Leaning over the bed*) Or a tailor. 'A suit from Pittorini's will last you a lifetime.'

SAM: Does it matter what he did?

TONY: I think it does, Samuel. I think Mr Pittorini is the contemporary equivalent of Yorrick's skull. Only now our memento moris are large scale. We keep the whole body, alive and yet not alive. I tell you this. Whatever he was he isn't now. Don't you think it's instructive to think of Mr Pittorini making phone calls, having it off with other people's wives, quarrelling with his neighbours, getting involved with community politics? All of it, when you think about it, completely and utterly pointless. All of it leading to his lying on a bed with fucking tubes up his nose. I mean, doesn't it make you think, Sammy? Doesn't it give you pause for thought? (*Pause.*) If Mr Pittorini had known he was going to end up like this he would have said to Mrs Pittorini – Assuming there was a Mrs Pittorini – 'Stuff it, Mrs Pittorini. Let's forget about the mortgage and the kids and our responsibilities. Let's blow all our savings on a cruise. Let's get-a laid, Mrs-a Pittorini while-a there's-a time.'

SAM: (*Humouring him – but almost drawn into the game*) Perhaps he wasn't married. Perhaps he was gay.

TONY: Very likely. He looks a bit gay.

SAM: But suppressed.

TONY: A closet.

SAM: Maybe.

TONY: Maybe he had a wasted life anyway. Maybe he never did anything of any interest. Maybe this is the most exciting thing that ever happened to him, lying on a bed in a hospital with tubes up his nose. (*Looking at him more closely*) Do you think he is actually dead?

SAM: Wouldn't they be able to tell? This is a hospital.

TONY: No one's been round for ages.

SAM: Is he –

TONY: He looks pretty fucking dead to me.

33

SAM: Is he breathing?

TONY: It's hard to tell.

SAM: (*Trying to withdraw*) Tony we can't –

TONY: Drop something. See if he starts.

SAM: Tony –

TONY: Cough.

SAM: Look –

TONY: I'll walk past. Casually. And cough.

SAM: Look –

(TONY *passes by the bed. An elaborate pantomime.*)
Well?

TONY: Impossible to tell.

SAM: Do you carry on like this to cheer yourself up, Tony? Is it because you're afraid of dying?

TONY: I'm afraid of other people dying. I want to go first. Before everyone else. I don't want to be upstaged.

SAM: Shall we have another shot? Shall we have another go at the old bugger?

TONY: I don't know what to do, Sammy. I've run out of things. I can't get my act together. Even talking. You see? Even the sacred bloody play-acting he and I always went in for. No good. (*Showing his fear and despair for the first time*) I've been up every day this week and I've pulled out all the old stops. Done the lot, you know? Will to live. Jesus, she doesn't know the half of it. I've run through all his great performances. I've done him doing Lear, I've done me watching him do Lear, I've done – (*Desperate*) There's nothing more I can say. I can feel it in the room. I can feel death in the room. I've done my act and still it won't go away. It's sitting on that bed there, looking across at him, grinning and feeling the edge of its razor. And all of the things I've thought were beautiful or clever or important about life. They won't help it to go away. It doesn't care you see. I tell it I'm a Labour Party supporter. I tell it I'm against Cruise. I tell it I'm a family man. I tell it I was the Most Promising Playwright of 1973. But it doesn't want to know, Sammy. It sits there on that bed turning over that old cut-throat razor, just like the one he had in the

34

bathroom, remember? And it won't go away. I've told it I'm sorry for being conceited and loud-mouthed and insensitive. I've apologized for tormenting a boy called Forster in form 3A at a public school in North London in 1964. But death isn't interested. I'm scared, Sammy. That's how things are with me at the moment. I am absolutely fucking terrified.

SAM: You'll be fine.

TONY: Will you take care of it? Is that it? Do I wind up running round the ward after you shouting 'Sammee – Sammee' like when we were kids, is that it? Will you think of something? You were great when my rabbit died, I remember. I seem to remember you telling me it had gone to heaven. Very forcefully.

SAM: I've lost a lot of edge since then. I was 12. I peaked at 12. (*Pause.*) You're right, though. We don't seem to be doing it, do we?

TONY: There's only one person who could.

SAM: Who's that?

TONY: Why does she stick us in the front line, Samuel? Because she's avoiding the issue. She won't bloody do it for him, that's why. And it isn't us he wants. It's her. It always was her. But she never gave herself, did she?

SAM: You'd do it so much better I suppose if you were married to him. Sometimes I think this fag act is for real.

TONY: Me too.

SAM: The reason I didn't come, Tony, is because I knew how much she'd lean on me. She never would lean on you that way, would she? I mean maybe you're right. Maybe it's all her bloody fault. Maybe if you love people enough they live for ever, I don't know. All I know is that she wants me to do it for her. I know that. I can't abandon her to him, do you see what I mean? I can see it all very very clearly. Which is why I never feel anything really, I suppose. (*Pause.*) I remember when Joan had the first baby. There I was in my white jacket, hunched over the table – out she came, blood sweat screams, the lot. 'Would you like to hold the baby, Mr Stone?' And I thought – 'So what? So fucking

35

what? It's only another baby.' (*Pause*.) I've got a mistress.
That's why my wife left. I've got this mistress. I've had her
for years.

TONY: Great.

SAM: In a little house. I've bought her this house. By the sea. I
don't think she particularly wanted to live by the sea but I
bought it anyway. So I go down there to . . . you know . . .

TONY: Well, you would, wouldn't you?

SAM: Yes . . . yes . . . I go down there and I . . . well.
Sometimes twice. Or three times. Or four. And I say
things . . . Like –

TONY: Hullo.

SAM: I talk about our relationship, you know. But I think I've
painted myself into a corner rather, I mean I'm fine, fine,
but . . .

TONY: What's her name?

SAM: Raquel.

TONY: She sounds just your sort of bird.

SAM: That's just the trouble with her.

TONY: You need someone to take you out of yourself.

SAM: Yeah . . .

TONY: Like me . . .

SAM: Oh. Yeah . . .

TONY: I'd like a mistress.

SAM: You can have mine. When I've finished with her.

TONY: Do you remember that? If she gave you anything I was
allowed a go. But not while it was new. For a week it was
this sacred thing called 'new' and then when it was no
longer 'new' then I was allowed in. And of course it felt
used up and not really what I wanted at all. I wanted it for
that first week, you see. I wanted to be you having it.

SAM: I don't remember that at all.

TONY: I wish he'd wake up.

SAM: So what are we –

TONY: I'll go and get her.

SAM: Tony –

TONY: It's got to be gone through, Samuel. Look at him. I
know what's been happening. She's never tried. She's gone

through the motions. But she's never actually tried. And until she does he's going to go on, retreating, an inch at a time, further away from the light. The way he retreated all his bloody life. Because she let him. Because she wouldn't love him enough. Don't you see that? And I tell you this – it isn't a piece of whimsy, it's hard fact, Samuel. If you don't love people they die.

SAM: They die when you love them sometimes. (*Pause.*) I will say this. I never felt I came out of love. I never felt I was here out of love. Maybe that's why there's no love in my life, I don't know. Maybe there was love once and it died. I don't know. But I'm afraid. If you really want to know, I'm afraid. If he's decided he wants to die then –

TONY: Then fine. Fine. I'm going to get her.

SAM: Don't –

TONY: I'm going to get her, Sammy. I'm going to make her bloody talk to him. Not the way she always did. Like he was some troublesome piece of furniture. But as if he was a person. Understand that? The will to live. The will to live for what?

SAM: She's old, Tony. They're both old. They get tired. They don't want –

TONY: They don't want to live. They want to die. They want their real feelings to wither like leaves on a tree. They want out. They want to avoid the issue. They want to say anything but what is in their hearts. But they mustn't be allowed to. They've got to say what they feel and whether they love or whether they hate and they've got to be bloody made to see that life is too precious to be allowed to slip away.

SAM: And are you so honest, Tony? Is this the way you live? All the time?

TONY: I –

SAM: It sounds tiring.

TONY: Do you want him to die?

SAM: Don't ask lawyers' questions.

TONY: Do you?

SAM: I – (*Pause.*) Isn't that what you're on the earth for, boy?

37

TONY: 'It's what you're on earth for, boy'?

> (TONY *does his father rather better than* SAM. *They look across at the sleeping old man with some tenderness.*)

SAM: Get her then. But go easy, can't you? Go easy.

TONY: Why?

SAM: (*A little threatening*) You could get hurt as well, I suppose.

TONY: I'm invulnerable to her. She can't do anything to me.

SAM: Maybe I'll do it for her.

TONY: I wonder whether he had any children.

SAM: Who?

TONY: Pittorini.

SAM: Leave Pittorini alone, can't you?

TONY: No. I won't leave any of it alone. I won't leave you alone and I won't leave her alone and I won't leave him alone and I certainly won't leave Mr Pittorini alone. Because all any of you want to do is to die. And I won't let you.

SAM: GO ON THEN! BLOODY JESUS CHRIST ON WHEELS! GO ON THEN! MAKE IT BLOODY WORSE THAN IT IS JUST SO AS YOU CAN FEEL! YOU DON'T FEEL ONLY WHEN IT HURTS, YOU KNOW!

TONY: LOOK, I TELL YOU WHAT I WANT –

> (MRS STONE *comes in through door.*)

MRS STONE: Oh.

TONY: Hi, Mom!

MRS STONE: Hullo. (*Pause.*) Were you . . .

TONY: Going? No.

MRS STONE: I was wondering.

TONY: I think we ought to stay.

MRS STONE: Oh.

TONY: Yes.

MRS STONE: I see.

TONY: It might help.

MRS STONE: I see.

TONY: And you –

MRS STONE: What?

TONY: If you –

MRS STONE: What?

TONY: I don't know. If you talked to him . . .

MRS STONE: What about, Anthony?

TONY: Everything.

MRS STONE: Oh. (*Pause.*) I'm a bit tired.

TONY: Yes.

MRS STONE: Sammy –

TONY: Do you see what I mean?

MRS STONE: Not really.

TONY: He'll wake up.

MRS STONE: Yes. (*Pause.*) Talk. (*Pause.*) Yes.

(*She starts to cry. SAM goes and puts his arm round her. TONY goes away to the other side of the bed.*)

I thought I'd –

SAM: What, Mum?

MRS STONE: I thought I'd finished for today, you see.

TONY: We haven't started yet, Mum. We haven't really started yet.

(*Slow fade on the figures.*)

As before. Figures as they were.

MRS STONE: Has he had his tea?

TONY: You what?

MRS STONE: Has he had his tea? His tea?

TONY: Ask him.

MRS STONE: I don't expect so. They're probably bringing it round. (*Pause.*) He won't eat, you see.

SAM: No?

MRS STONE: (*Totally preoccupied*) He won't eat. For three days. And he says if they put him on a drip he'll . . . well, he won't, you see . . . (*Pause.*) You have to feed him.

TONY: Yes?

MRS STONE: And mash it up like a baby.

TONY: Ahhh.

MRS STONE: He doesn't like it, you see. He won't co-operate.

TONY: We gathered that.

MRS STONE: I brought him a banana.

TONY: Magic.

MRS STONE: Yesterday I brought him a banana. And when I got home it had got all over things in my bag. It had disintegrated completely, this banana. It was all in bits.

TONY: So what did you do?

MRS STONE: I had to cut it off.

TONY: And then what did you do?

SAM: (*Irritated again*) Tony –

TONY: I'm just riveted to the story of this banana. I'm on the edge of my seat to know how it all turned out. I'm amazed at the breath-taking drama you can impart to the smallest thing, Mother.

MRS STONE: I had the same thing with a yoghurt pot.

TONY: *No*.

MRS STONE: Yes. I'd brought him a yoghurt pot. With raspberry yoghurt in it. And I put it on the bed and he just stared at it as if it had done something awful. Which is odd because he likes yoghurt. He really is very fond of yoghurt. And then, after a while, he just said, in that great deep voice of his, like a bear – 'Take it away.' So – I popped it into my bag and –

TONY: Don't tell me, don't tell me. It leaked.

MRS STONE: How did you know?

TONY: Intuition.

MRS STONE: On Monday I brought him a piece of cheese. And –

TONY: FOR GOD'S SAKE!

(MR STONE *starts awake*.)

MR STONE: Uh?

MRS STONE: Hullo . . .

MR STONE: What?

MRS STONE: It's me.

MR STONE: What?

MRS STONE: I –

(MR STONE *slips back to sleep*.)

TONY: I'm going to talk to Mr Pittorini. I'll get more sense out of Mr Pittorini.

MRS STONE: Have you been talking to Mr Pittorini?

TONY: Oh, yes. I've been talking about Cruise missiles and Gay Rights and the Third World. I've really been rapping with Mr Pittorini. We're like that are me and Mr Pittorini.

MRS STONE: Oh. (*Pause.*) Good. (*Pause.*) I sometimes think they understand you know. Even though you don't seem to get response, I think they understand.

TONY: Italians, you mean?

MRS STONE: Disabled.

TONY: Disabled Italians, you mean.

MRS STONE: I meant –

TONY: Why is it that talking to anyone in this family is like talking to a brick wall?

SAM: You what?

MRS STONE: Well, then. I suppose we better –

TONY: No.

MRS STONE: What?

TONY: Staying. We're staying.

MRS STONE: I was here at ten, lovey. I was here at ten. (*Pause.*) After a while there's not much you can say. You just sit there, you see. And watch. And wait. And he might say something. Or he might not. And after a while he says, in that great deep voice of his, 'You run along.' And you run along. There's really not much to say. (*Pause.*) I say to him, 'You've got to get better. You've got your work to think about. You've always loved acting.' He always did love acting.

TONY: I know. Well, he was an actor, wasn't he?

MRS STONE: 'And you'll recover . . .' You know?

TONY: Yes.

MRS STONE: '. . . and –'

TONY: Act.

MRS STONE: Yes. (*Pause.*) But he just sits there. That's why I thought you might . . . I brought him some yoghurt.

TONY: You told us about the yoghurt.

SAM: Tony –

MRS STONE: Did I? Oh. (*Pause.*) What else do I say? Oh. I tell him about the garden. The garden's in a terrible state. I tell him about Frank next door. I read the papers, you know. To him. Tell him the news. But he doesn't seem to want to hear the news. He's got no interest in current affairs at the moment.

TONY: Maybe you don't read with enough expression –

SAM: Look – you said –

TONY: I know what I said.

MRS STONE: He doesn't show much enthusiasm for the reviews. He used to really like the reviews. I mean they made him mad but he did enjoy the reviews. But now they seem to mean absolutely nothing to him.

TONY: Mr Pittorini loves the reviews. You should read the reviews to Mr Pittorini. He's dying to hear what they have to say. He was on the boards, you know.

MRS STONE: Was he?

SAM: Tony –

TONY: 'PITTORINI A SENSATION IN LEAR.'

MRS STONE: Was he?

TONY: 'ELOQUENT PERFORMANCE FROM PITTORINI IN SHAW REVIVAL.' Sir Oswald Pittorini. I saw him many a time and oft. At the Rialto.

MRS STONE: You're taking the mickey out of me.

TONY: You're right. I am.

MRS STONE: What do you want me to say to him?

TONY: Why didn't you sleep together for twenty years?

SAM: For God's sake Tony –

MRS STONE: (*She didn't hear – she never does when she doesn't want to.*) You what?

TONY: Did somebody say something? Did anyone speak? I didn't hear anything. Did someone ask a direct question? I don't think so. I'm sure not.

MRS STONE: We met at a production at the local theatre. I'd been told this young man was worth seeing. I wasn't really interested actually.

TONY: In what?

MRS STONE: Men, I suppose. (*Pause.*) Well, he was there and he had this deep bass voice.

TONY: 'What's up with you, boy?'

MRS STONE: And he asked me to go out with him. And he had this voice and . . .

TONY: Is that it?

MRS STONE: There isn't much else I want to say, Anthony. People like us don't, do we? We just don't like to discuss our emotions. That may be wrong but that's the way we are. We're just an ordinary English family, aren't we, really? That's all we are. And you're part of us, Anthony. Even if you pretend not to be. Even if we are theatrical we're only a *bit* theatrical. He did quite a lot of radio actually.

TONY: I was born under a cabbage leaf in Dalston Junction. It says so in my programme notes. Dunnit. Cunt.

SAM: Tony thinks we don't show emotion because we haven't any emotions to show.

MRS STONE: I don't think that's true. I think we have a lot of emotions. About all sorts of things. But we prefer not to put them on display. (*Pause.*) He used to shout at the television. Shout at it. He'd get up and scream at the announcers. Especially the announcers. They'd just sit there and say, 'Goodnight' or 'Hullo' or 'Sleep well' and he'd shout this most foul language at them.

TONY: Wake him up. Talk to him. Go on. Wake him up.

MRS STONE: Tony –

TONY: I want you to wake him up. And talk to him. He looks dead like that. I can't stand it. If you don't wake him up I'll start –

(*But* SAM, *seeing how strung up* TONY *is by the first sign of his* MOTHER *fighting back, is shaking their* FATHER.)

SAM: Father –

MR STONE: Uh?

SAM: Dad –

MR STONE: Uh?

SAM: Mum's here . . .

MR STONE: Uh?

SAM: Mum's here.

MR STONE: You what?

MRS STONE: I'm here.

MR STONE: Oh.

MRS STONE: I came back.

MR STONE: Yes?

MRS STONE: Are you all right?

MR STONE: Yes. (*Pause.*) You go.

MRS STONE: I might . . .

MR STONE: Might what?

MRS STONE: I thought I might stay for a bit.

MR STONE: Oh. (*Pause.*) Why?

MRS STONE: I just –

TONY: Talk. Chat chat chat chat. Rabbit rabbit rabbit. You know. Have fun. Celebrate. Live. Proclaim the meaningfulness of your partnership.

MR STONE: What's the boy talking about?

MRS STONE: I don't know, dear.

MR STONE: Haven't the faintest. Never had the faintest. Saw one of his plays once. Completely incomprehensible. Man

44

in a donkey jacket saying unspeakable things. I said,
'What's this play of yours about, boy?' He said, 'It's about
the Industrial Relations Bill.' 'Oh, well, never mind,' I
said. I ask you. Is that a fit subject for drama?

TONY: Anything's a fit subject for drama.

MR STONE: It is for you, boy.

TONY: It is for you, Dad.

MR STONE: Is it?

TONY: 'Pass the toast.'

MR STONE: The what?

TONY: 'The toast.'

MR STONE: This is incomprehensible.

(*In fact* MR STONE's *manner is quite as dramatic as* TONY's
parody.)

TONY: 'I am on my knees. I beseech you. I implore you to pass
the toast.'

MR STONE: You implore me to what, boy? 'I tell you –'

TONY: Don't stop, Dad. Go on. Don't stop. Please.

MR STONE: Tony, you –

TONY: Maybe you're right, Samuel. Maybe all I do is set people
up. Get them to go through routines. My routines usually.
Involving things like . . . oh . . . Faith . . . Hope. You
know? Maybe I don't believe it any more than anyone else.
It's just good business for my characters to say it. 'Tony
Stone cannot spell, cannot put a paragraph together, he has
about as much idea of how to write dialogue as a prune.
But. But. He has compassion.' But what is this
compassion? Maybe there isn't any such thing. Maybe
you're more honest than I am. Maybe you know there's just
a big black hole in the ground waiting for all of us.

MR STONE: What's the boy saying?

MRS STONE: I don't understand him.

SAM: He's talking about himself as usual.

TONY: Listen you –

MRS STONE: He was all right till we put him in his pram
outside. That's where we went wrong with Tony. Inside he
was fine. But as soon as he was outside he got ever so
naughty. And from then on you couldn't do anything with

45

him. We should have kept him inside.

TONY: For thirty-three years. Why when one tries to persuade one's parents to talk to each other for the first time for twenty years do they end up discussing oneself?

MRS STONE: Well, it's all there is to talk about. In a way. You'll understand. When you're older.

TONY: Well, Mother, Ella and I won't have anything to discuss. Or did you forget? Had that little incident slipped your mind.

(*He does an impression of his daughter at her. A nasty moment.* SAM *comes in quickly.*)

SAM: So where did I go wrong, then?

TONY: Jesus!

MRS STONE: You were a Truby King baby. That's where you went wrong, I think.

SAM: A Truby what?

MRS STONE: There was this person called Truby King. He was ever so famous. It was all the rage. You had to do it the way Truby King did it. He was *the* thing, you know?

SAM: What was he? A singer?

MRS STONE: He was a doctor. He believed babies should be put down to sleep. Not held. Put in a cot. And fed every four hours. Only every four hours. Even if they were screaming with hunger you weren't supposed to pick them up.

SAM: My God. Was he a German?

MRS STONE: I don't think so.

SAM: And did you do this to me?

MRS STONE: I tried to.

SAM: Dear oh dear.

MRS STONE: I used to stand outside your room crying and looking at my watch. 'There's still a quarter of an hour to go,' he used to say. 'You can't pick him up yet.' (*Pause.*) It was hopeless really. I don't think there were any *real* Truby King babies. There were just lots of attempts at it. I mean any mother who was a mother and not a machine always ended picking the baby up, you see. But I think Truby King said that if you didn't let them go the full four hours, then the whole thing had gone wrong and you'd end up

with a sort of monster baby, one that wasn't yours and
wasn't Truby King's. A sort of half-and-half affair. And so,
when the baby wouldn't eat its food or had a temper or bit
you on the leg or something then it was all your fault, not
Truby King's.

TONY: Why do families like ours live our lives out of books?
Why do we spend our time looking for rules to obey?

SAM: Here we go again. Why can't we all be as natural as bus
conductors?

TONY: I suppose because we spend our lives telling other people
what to do we need orders for ourselves.

SAM: You're the expert on giving orders, aren't you though?
You spend your life telling cowed Japanese tourists What is
Wrong with Britain. As if you knew anything about Britain
or what is wrong with it. All you do is sit in a room all day.
I'm out there. I see it.

TONY: Well, you tell me what's wrong with Britain then.

SAM: You'd probably put it in a play. You have absolutely no
scruples.

TONY: It probably wouldn't be good enough to put in a play.

SAM: I'll tell you what is wrong with Britain. What we have got
is a discrepancy in what we economists call the Demand
Function. People, in other words, want things. And our
job, as economists and leaders of society, is to make sure
they don't get them. So, what we've got to do is to get all
the things they want, all the tellies and washing-up
machines and electric kettles and hatchbacks and video
recorders and take them out to the middle of Salisbury
Plain and bury them deep in the earth.

TONY: What happens then?

SAM: Then you get something that we economists call Demand
Drop, i.e. massive redundancies, misery, deaths, despair
and retreat into barbarity. So then we go back to Salisbury
Plain and dig up the tellies and the washing-up machines
and the hatchbacks and the video recorders and start all
over again, with the important difference that at least this
time the bastards will be a little bit grateful.

TONY: That's quite good. Can't quite see how to –

47

SAM: Use it. But . . .

TONY: But . . . (*Pause.*) I was always supposed to be the funny and clever one. God knows why. You were twice as funny. Three times as clever. If you would only let yourself be. But the family seemed to close in on you, seemed to dry up all feeling, so that person I knew was there, underneath all that, never flowered in the way it did when we were kids. So that I'd look at you in some neutral place and think 'My God. That dull middle-aged man can't be him. That can't be Sammy. Surely not.'

SAM: I'm touched that you take such an interest in my essential dullness.

TONY: He's gone to sleep.

MRS STONE: We better leave him.

TONY: Mum – we've already left him out. I feel we never did include him. I feel we haven't loved him enough and that's why he's dying. I feel you haven't loved him enough and that's why he's dying. I want to include him. Don't you think, Mum? I want him with us. You understand?

(MRS STONE *is crying.*)

I don't want to be cruel. I'm just saying what's in my heart.

SAM: Well, don't. Don't. Don't. Don't.

MRS STONE: Tony –

SAM: I'M BORED WITH WHAT'S IN YOUR HEART! I DON'T WANT TO HEAR IT ANY MORE!

MRS STONE: Tony –

TONY: All I want is the answer to a simple question. A very simple question. It's always *us* who has to approach him, isn't it? All I want to know is –

MRS STONE: Please, Tony –

TONY: All I want to know is 'Do you love him?' That's all. Do you love him? Have you ever loved him? Haven't I the right to know that? Haven't I?

MRS STONE: I don't know. I don't know whether you have the right to know that. I don't have the answers to any of your questions. (*Pause.*) Do you love Ella? Does she love you?

TONY: Yes.

SAM: He said in a faltering voice.

48

TONY: Leave it out.

MRS STONE: Is it so perfect with you? You never let me near her. Or your child. Why? If it was all so perfect, why?

TONY: We're talking about –

SAM: We're talking about you, Tony.

TONY: I wish he'd wake up.

SAM: You, Tony.

TONY: He's shamming.

SAM: 'Answer your mother.'

TONY: Mum –

MRS STONE: Well –

TONY: You never wanted to come near her. You hardly ever spoke to her.

MRS STONE: When little Alison died, I –

TONY: WE'RE NOT HERE TO TALK ABOUT ALISON! WE'RE HERE TO TALK ABOUT YOU! (*Pause.*) Let the dead bury their dead. Even if he is seventy-four years older than she was, at least he's still alive. She was barely alive. She hadn't learned to sing or dance or walk or crawl before death came along. Before she met that nice young man with the razor I was telling you about, sitting on the corner of that bed and waiting for one of us. She thought he was fine probably. I bet death is really good with children. He talks to them and chucks them under the chin and they go quietly, quietly . . .

MRS STONE: Listen –

TONY: There he is. There he is. (*Crossing to a vacant bed*) Out, you. Visiting hour is over. Out. Out.

SAM: Tony –

TONY: Well, please don't either of you ask me personal questions about my life when you couldn't even be bothered to come to my daughter's funeral. I mean, I know it was a small funeral. As a life it hadn't really got off the ground. She was a bit . . . (*Does gibbering impression.*) Never even made the second birthday. We thought about burying her in the garden next to the guinea-pig. But it was, in the end, a real live funeral and you couldn't be bothered to show up so I think that means that you are not

in the least interested in my life and have not the right to
ask me any personal questions, so can you both shut up
about me and my wife, who neither of you can stand, and
get on with the business that has brought us here and is the
only reason why we are exchanging words at all, i.e.
keeping Sir Herbert Beerbohm Tree there out of *The Times*
obituary column.

MRS STONE: I never came because I was never asked.

TONY: You don't ask people to funerals.

MRS STONE: I mean I wasn't –

TONY: Talking to us. And we weren't talking to you. And he
wasn't talking to me. And I wasn't talking to Joan and Joan
had never talked to Ella and he had never talked to Joan,
Ella Sam, me, or indeed you or indeed anyone for the last
twenty years. Too fucking right we're an ordinary English
middle-class family. No one ever talks to anyone about
anything. Ever.

SAM: You do your best to make up for it. We're great listeners.

MRS STONE: You always were one for talking.

TONY: I like some response occasionally. (*Over to* MR
PITTORINI) 'Don't I, Mr Pittorini?' 'Yes-a, you do.'

SAM: She asked whether you loved Ella.

TONY: Of course I love Ella. She's my wife. You disapprove of
her. Therefore I love her. I asked her whether she loved –

MRS STONE: Forty-seven years, Anthony. Forty-seven years.
I've been with him for forty-seven years.

TONY: What do you want? A medal? I didn't ask you how long
you'd been with him, I asked –

MRS STONE: That's all there is. Time is all there is. There's a
day and another day and after that yet another day and
suddenly your children are shouting at you and telling you
things you thought you knew already. Forty-seven years,
that's all I'm saying. (*Pause.*) What does it mean, anyway?
This love you're talking about. Doesn't it just mean being
with someone and looking after them? Caring for them?

TONY: It ought to mean a lot more than that. You make it
sound like agency nursing. There's a scale for love. Like
the Richter scale. There are degrees of it, like Réaumur or

Centigrade. It can be measured in inches, feet, yards, rods, poles, perches, by volume weight. Imperial measures, gallons, pints, quarters, in pounds avoirdupois, in square areas, acres of love or – (*Stops.*) I don't know. Love is what you want to feel but don't. What you try to feel. I don't *know*. But I do know that it's more than carting around yoghurt pots and clocking up forty-seven years. Forty-seven years of what? Of ignoring someone? Forty-seven years of nothing.

SAM: I warned you . . .

TONY: Yeah.

SAM: Right . . .

TONY: Big brother squares up. Right?

(TERRY *comes in with a card menu.*)

TERRY: Dinnertime.

MRS STONE: Oh, there you are, Terry.

TERRY: Will you give it to him, Mrs Stone?

MRS STONE: Is that the –

TERRY: That's what's on, Mrs Stone.

(MRS STONE *reads from the menu.*)

MRS STONE: (*Rather declamatory*) Quiche Lorraine.

TONY: We're trying to convince him it's worth staying alive.

TERRY: Of course you are.

MRS STONE: Chicken casserole.

TONY: Only we seem to be a bit short on things that make it worth staying alive.

MRS STONE: Sultana pudding.

(MR STONE *is stirring into wakefulness.*)

SAM: There's a reason for living.

MRS STONE: Fruit salad. Or cheese and biscuits.

(MR STONE *isn't responding.*)

Chicken?

(*Still nothing.*)

Quiche Lorraine? (*Pause.*) Well, let me get them to bring something. Cake. I could bring some cake later. You like cake.

MR STONE: Do I?

MRS STONE: Quiche Lorraine and fruit salad, please.

TERRY: Right y'are, Mrs Stone.

TONY: And two helpings of sultana pudding for Mr Pittorini.

TERRY: Listen, young man. With your mother here and –

TONY: Everything –

TERRY: Just take it easy. OK?

TONY: OK, Terence. (*As he is going*) Do you suppose he's gay? Quite a lot of faggots go in for nursing, you know.

MRS STONE: He's awfully nice. (*To her* HUSBAND) They've got the menu for tomorrow. You can choose. There's eggs Florentine. There's beef Stifado. There's buck rabbit. Tomorrow.

MR STONE: No.

MRS STONE: And afterwards there's chocolate pudding. There's ice-cream. And there's apple pie. Which you can have with custard or not, you see.

MR STONE: No.

MRS STONE: Oh, have a little bit of apple pie. At least have a bit of apple pie. Have something. If you can't have beef Stifado or eggs Florentine or buck rabbit, at least have a bit of apple pie. At least have some of that.

MR STONE: No.

MRS STONE: It's tomorrow. It's not today. You don't have to eat it now. But by tomorrow you may be ready for it.

MR STONE: No. (*Pause.*) I wanted to say something. To all of you.

TONY: What, Dad?

MR STONE: It's very important. It –

SAM: What? What did you want to say?

MR STONE: I – (*Struggling through the disability*) Beef Stifado. What's that when it's at home? What I wanted to say was – (*Pause.*) The thing one wants to say is never the thing one says. And when one comes to the pitch of saying it, it sounds . . . mawkish or clumsy, or . . . the words in your heart are never the words on your lips. The thing I want to say is . . . (*Pause.*) I hear things. I hear voices. You're arguing. It's like a play. Like watching a play. I can't . . . (*Pause.*)

TONY: It bloody is desperate.

MRS STONE: Darling –

MR STONE: You what? (*He seems not to recognize her*)

MRS STONE: Should we get the doctor, Sam?

TONY: We've had the bloody doctor, Mum. What did the doctor say? He said his temperature was stable. He said a whole load of rubbish. He said, to all intents and purposes, that if Dad wanted to die he wasn't going to come between him and the experience. Modern medicine. 'If dying's what you need at this time.' Look at him. He's slipping away. Minute by minute further and further out. Hold on to him. Talk to him about –

MRS STONE: About what?

TONY: About the day the bomb fell on your wedding reception. About the time you packed a suitcase and went down to – (*Desperate*) Come on . . .

(*But* MR STONE *is asleep again. She is holding his hand.*)

SAM: You can't separate yourself, Tony. Their stories are your stories. However much you try to deny yourself and deny us you're a part of us. You're part of an ordinary English family. That's all you are. All you are. (*Vicious*) And we were talking about you. And your marriage. And your little house.

TONY: It's quite a big house.

SAM: Weren't we?

TONY: Why are you so fucking persistent?

SAM: Because I'm your brother. And I know you. And I'm not going to let you get away with it. I'm not going to let you go on hurting people in the name of some phoney 'honesty'.

TONY: You can talk about honesty. You took her side all the way, didn't you, in the Ella business? Did just what Mummy wanted, didn't you? You'll always be running her errands. Well, even if you couldn't be bothered to –

SAM: You, Tony. We were talking about you. Not how you choose to present yourself. But how others see you. You're very very frank and honest about the rest of us, aren't you? Well, now let's try some of the same treatment on you, shall we?

TONY: And what shall we talk about?

SAM: The very thing you don't want to talk about. This wonderful wonderful relationship that's the envy of the world. This woman you love so much and with whom you are so fearless and honest. I don't believe it, Tony. I don't believe a word of it. I think it's just as dead on its feet as everything else in this family. I think you lie about it because you want to look good. I think you attack me and her because of the terrible bloody lie in your own life.

TONY: Listen –

(TERRY *comes in with a tray of food.*)

Do you do a cabaret act as well, Terence?

(TERRY *ignores him and carries the tray over to* MRS STONE.)

I mean, is there anyone else in this hospital apart from you? I mean, I know they're cutting back on the National Health but this is ridiculous. Do you run out there and grab a chef's hat and do the meals? Do you do operations as well? Do you clean the floors and run the administrative side of things? I mean, is there anyone left in this place apart from you? Are you the entire staff?

TERRY: We're understaffed.

TONY: What are the other buggers doing?

TERRY: There you are, Mr Stone.

MR STONE: 'Kyou.

TONY: You don't have to shout at him, Terence. He can hear you perfectly well. He just doesn't want to, that's all. He –

TERRY: WILL YOU SHUT IT, PLEASE? WILL YOU JUST – (*Checks himself.*) I'm sorry, Mrs Stone.

MRS STONE: That's all right, Terry.

TERRY: Long day. I just . . .

MRS STONE: Terry, it isn't your fault. We're all a bit –

TONY: Tired.

TERRY: I'm sorry.

TONY: Please don't be. I just wanted to see you behave in an unprofessional manner.

TERRY: I was just –

TONY: I just can't stand the way you look at me, you see. I'm sorry. I can't stand it. You look as if you're sizing up for bereavement.

54

TERRY: I was just –

TONY: And you don't like me. I can see that too. You think I'm an affected, unfeeling, half-baked little slob, don't you? I'm just not your type. I could see that the first day I walked in.

SAM: Tony –

TERRY: Listen. I'm sorry I shouted at you.

TONY: Don't be sorry. Please don't be sorry. I can't stand it. You look so bloody sorry for me. I can't bear it, I'm afraid.

TERRY: I'm sorry. I can't help it. You –

TONY: I what?

TERRY: You love him a lot, don't you?

TONY: Amazing insight . . .

TERRY: And you want him all to yourself, I think.

TONY: A psychiatrist as well!

SAM: I thought you were all for the direct expression of opinion.

TONY: Only when the opinion is one I agree with.

TERRY: I shouldn't have shouted like that. I'm sorry.

TONY: Do they ring a bell?

TERRY: When?

TONY: To let you know it's over. Visiting.

TERRY: There's no bell. You stay as long as you want.

TONY: I would have liked a bell. Why don't they send a doctor round? Why is he in this outhouse? Why have they given up on him? Why doesn't he hold on? Why is he slipping away? Why – (*Pause.*) He's dying, isn't he?

TERRY: If he's not careful.

TONY: I can feel it. Inch by inch. Letting go.

TERRY: I'll be back later, Mrs Stone. For the tray.

MRS STONE: Thank you, Terry.

TONY: I wish they'd ring a bell. You know? To tell us when to stop feeling like this. We only want to be machines, that's all. We're just an ordinary English family. All we ask is to feel absolutely nothing at all. That's not much to ask, is it?

TERRY: I'm sorry I shouted at you like that. It was a quite unforgivable thing to do.

TONY: WILL YOU PLEASE STOP LOOKING AT ME LIKE THAT? WILL YOU? I CAN'T STAND IT! WILL YOU?

TERRY: I'm sorry.

(*He goes.*)

TONY: I don't think he's gay. I think he's straight.

MRS STONE: Darling . . . it's some tea . . . darling . . .

SAM: So this incredible wife of yours, Tony, for which you forsook us all.

TONY: You don't let go, do you?

SAM: This real world you live in. As opposed to the ashcan of history into which we have been dumped.

TONY: Off the North Circular Road.

SAM: How do you manage? How is it in this wonderful radical paradise in which you live, where all your friends have the same opinions and all *care* about each other and Black people and the Bomb and the NHS. I mean, what's it like? What's it like to be so appallingly, smugly complacent? I just want to know.

TONY: About what?

SAM: About Ella. I want to know all about her. She's a Greenham woman I take it. She must be a Greenham woman these days. Got to be. Legwarmers? Has she got the legwarmers? Does she go on about 'the feeling among the women'. Does she go on about the immense peace and spiritual calm she feels among the *women*? That's all they're in it for, isn't it? The women. Christ, if I went on about 'the men' the way they go on about 'the women' I'd be carted off straight away. 'I knew as the bitter ale washed over my tongue, I knew as I saw the brawny arms of those around me, that I was among the men. I was part of the men, a great tide of *man* swept me up in its maleness.' They'd have me down for a faggot straight off, wouldn't they?

TONY: You've never been interested in Ella. She has never existed for you, has she? She has never really been here. You just look straight through her. I don't think you understand one thing about her.

SAM: And you do?

TONY: Oh, come off it.

SAM: Well, is she? Is she the be-all and end-all for you?

56

TONY: Listen –

SAM: Is she?

MRS STONE: PLEASE! (*Pause.*) Please, boys. I'm trying to get him to –

SAM: I'm sorry, Mum.

TONY: We're fine, Samuel. We're just fine.

SAM: It's all perfect, is it? It's a life-enhancing –

TONY: We're fine.

SAM: Does she have affairs, Tone? Does she –

MRS STONE: Please, Sammy.

TONY: Don't interrupt him, Mum. He's about your business. He's doing his best to bring your little boy back to the fold. Away from that nasty woman who stole him away from you. He's doing his best to make me your little boy again the way he always was and always will be which is why he can't make any kind of relationship with any kind of woman, even one in a trouser suit. Oh, let him go on and on and on and on. I do very badly under interrogation. I may crack and own up to the fact that deep down it's Mummy I want. 'DO YOU LOVE YOUR VIFE?' 'VOT'S WRONG VISS YOUR MUZZER? YOU HEAR?'

MRS STONE: I was only trying to –

TONY: PLEASE DON'T GIVE ME ANY OF THAT SHIT! DON'T GIVE ME ANY OF THAT 'I TRIED' CRAP! DON'T TRY AND KID ME WITH THAT SOFT, INSISTENT VOICE OF YOURS THAT YOU DIDN'T WANT ME TO BE PRECISELY WHAT YOU WANTED! ADMIT IT! IF YOU HAD HAD YOUR WAY I'D STILL BE STAGGERING AROUND YOUR BACK GARDEN CARRYING YOUR FUCKING YOGHURT POTS FOR YOU! (*Pause.*) Only I got out. I escaped. (*Pause.*) I've never forgotten that day I left to go to Ella's. You stood at the door and looked at me and waved as if I was about to go off to the First World War. And I waved at you and I felt the tears prick at the back of my eyes.

MRS STONE: I loved you. That's all, Anthony. I just didn't want you to go off like that.

TONY: SHE ONLY LIVES IN FUCKING KILBURN, MUM! IT WASN'T MOULMEIN OR CARACAS! IT'S THREE STOPS AWAY ON THE FUCKING BAKERLOO LINE! WHAT DO YOU WANT, MUM?

MRS STONE: I want you to be happy.

TONY: WELL, I'M NOT HAPPY! LOOK! OK? I'M NOT HAPPY! HAPPY?

SAM: Why aren't you happy?

TONY: Shut your face.

(MR STONE *has woken up. He sees the food on the tray in front of him.*)

MR STONE: No.

MRS STONE: Please.

MR STONE: No.

MRS STONE: It's quiche. I've mashed it up. Please.

MR STONE: No.

MRS STONE: I've mashed it.

MR STONE: No.

(*She starts to cry.*)

SAM: Don't cry, Mum.

TONY: You can do what you like to her, Dad. You can ignore her or hit her or try a combination of the two but the one thing you must not do is refuse to eat.

MRS STONE: He won't . . . (*Sobbing*) He just won't, you see. None of it's any good.

TONY: It's the story of their marriage. She wants to and he doesn't. Or was it the other way around?

SAM: Shut up.

TONY: NO!

SAM: And how about you and Red Rosa, eh?

TONY: Don't call my wife Red Rosa.

SAM: Well, what do you call her?

TONY: I call her – (*Pause.*) I don't know. I –

SAM: His voice faltered.

TONY: I mean –

SAM: As he suddenly realized –

TONY: Why are you trying to trap me?

SAM: Because I suspect you. I suspect that things aren't as wonderful as you make out. The way things aren't as easy to solve as you and your smug radical friends think they are.

MRS STONE: Sammy.

SAM: Yes, Mum?

MRS STONE: Will you try?

SAM: Yes, Mum.

TONY: 'Yes, Mum.'

SAM: Don't go away. I'll be back.

TONY: I can hardly wait.

(SAM *crosses to his* FATHER.)

MR STONE: No.

SAM: Dad, they all say. You've got to eat.

MR STONE: No.

SAM: You must.

MR STONE: Must?

SAM: You won't –

MR STONE: Won't what?

SAM: Get well.

MR STONE: Well? Well? (*Pause.*) Never will get well. (*Pause.*)
It's my body, Sammy. I won't urge it any more. I won't put
it through its paces. I'm on the stage and the lights are . . .
you know . . . what lights do when they . . .

TONY: Fade.

MR STONE: Thank you.

SAM: You do it, then. You persuade him. You use all your talent
for persuading others that the world is a place capable of
improvement, use your passionate faith in the Rights of
Man and your proud championship of the working class to
persuade your father to eat a piece of quiche Lorraine? Eh?

TONY: OK.

SAM: We'll carry on from there.

MRS STONE: Please, boys. Please don't fight. I can't stand it
when you fight.

TONY: The last thirty years must have been difficult.

SAM: Plate?

TONY: Plate.

MR STONE: I said no.

(TONY *crosses to take over* SAM's *place.*)

TONY: I know. But. 'For me.' 'Do it for me.' That's what they
say to children, isn't it? She used to say it to me. 'For me.'
Every mouthful part of a psychological war. Well, don't do
it for me, Dad. Do it for yourself. (*Holding out plate*) There

59

it is. British Hospital Food. If you can eat that you can eat anything. It's a challenge. Go on. It won't be here for ever, you know. The way things are going in the National Health they won't be able to afford food soon. (*Quiet*) Eat it for yourself, Dad. Eat it for yourself. You will get better. But you must want to. The will. Remember that old thing? I don't think you ever had the chance to do what you wanted to do, did you? Weren't you just blown about by women and circumstances the way we all are. Well. We are the weaker sex. But now you can really start. Now you know what life is. Life is what Mr Pittorini has not got. What you very nearly lost. But now. Now you'll go to Paris. Play Lear. Get your own TV series. It all starts with a plate of mashed-up quiche Lorraine. (*Pause.*) Just a mouthful, Pater. Just a mouthful. One mouthful. Then – who knows? Just one. Then you'll be off and away. It's been three days, Dad. Please. They'll put you on a – (*Pause.*) Look. Just a crumb. A symbolic act. Holy Communion. Take this in remembrance of me. Just a crumb. (*Desperate*) COME ON!

MRS STONE: It's what I was telling you, Tony. He won't. Maybe it is me. Maybe it's all of us. Why doesn't he want to?

TONY: If this is the case, comrade parent. If this is the issue – (*Pause.*) I am staying here until I see that plate empty. I am going to be standing over you until I see a clean plate. Do you want chocolates? Well, if you don't have quiche you don't have chocolates. What's that? You don't want chocolates? That's cheating. Don't you want to grow up healthy and strong like the other boys? Don't you want to get married? Shame on you. You want to die? (*Close*) Listen – dying's awful. Dying's climbing into a black plastic bag and zipping it up over your head. Don't give me that resurrection and the life bit because I don't believe a word of it.

MR STONE: Don't you?

TONY: Listen, I like talking to you, OK? I like you fine as it happens. I don't fancy going to your funeral. I mean, you won't be there, will you? I like people who dribble. I just don't want you to die, you understand?

MR STONE: Yes.

TONY: Please. Eat the fucking thing. Please.

(MR STONE *shakes his head.*)

I'm getting cross now. I am getting really angry. Before I was just pretending to be cross but now I really am. Cross. Really cross.

MR STONE: I want to say something. I want –

TONY: You've got to make some effort before we –

MR STONE: Want to say that –

TONY: Allow you to say anything. We –

MR STONE: I wanted to say –

TONY: EAT IT! EAT IT, DAMN YOU! EAT IT! (*Pushing the plate at his father*) People have blessed the plain with the golden grain to get this made up for you. Packers have packed. Bakers have baked. Eat it. Stand up for your stomach. (*Close to tears*) Stand up for yourself, Dad. Stand up for yourself against them. The stupid bastards who said you couldn't act and who sniggered about your one gesture and the wife who didn't get what you were saying half the time and me too probably who went my own way and never listened to you. Stand up for yourself, Dad. The way you didn't that afternoon in our front hall twenty-five years ago as she said, 'I'm going out' and you said, 'Don't leave me' and she said, 'I'm going out' and your lower lip trembled and you started to cry, I've never forgotten it, Dad, never. I was on your side, Daddy. I still am. Get up. Please. Be like I wanted you to be then. Laying waste to all around you. For me. Please. (*Pushing the plate at him*) EAT THE FUCKING THING!

MRS STONE: TONY –

TONY: SHUT UP!

SAM: I wanted to say that –

TONY: (*Forcing the food down his mouth*) GET IT DOWN YOU!

SAM: TONY –

TONY: DON'T TURN YOUR HEAD AWAY! DON'T BACK AWAY FROM IT! ALL YOUR LIFE YOU WALKED AWAY FROM LIVING! YOU LET THEM WALK ALL OVER YOU, DAD! PLEASE DON'T TURN YOUR HEAD AWAY!

61

(SAM *gets to him. A scuffle.*)

MR STONE: I wanted to say that I don't want to . . .

TONY: Fight . . .

MR STONE: Anyone to fight. Don't want to . . .

TONY: See us fight.

MR STONE: I'm so tired, Tony. I've been so tired for so much of my life. Even up there on the stage with my one . . .

TONY: Gesture.

MR STONE: There's been a little voice at the back of my head, whispering –

TONY: No.

MR STONE: Whispering, 'No.' Whispering, 'Why bother?' You see. The thing I wanted to say was this. I don't want to . . . this . . . all this while this machine is to me . . . I don't want it to be . . . I don't want it . . . revels, you know . . . when they end . . . the thing that lights do at the end of a . . . show . . . all gone . . . want to be . . . free . . .
(*Fighting through the disability, suddenly sharp*) You won't let me alone, will you? Of all of them you're the one who sticks closest to me. Well, you must let me alone, darling. You must get on and do your work. Which is to . . .
describe . . . you know . . . describe the . . . lights . . .

TONY: They said –

MR STONE: I am not going to get well, Tony.

TONY: Your will –

MR STONE: My will is not to any longer.

TONY: You'll see. Don't be crazy. You'll see.
(*He has broken free of* SAM *and gone to his* FATHER.)
You'll see. Look. You'll be up there again. Jesus. You won't know yourself.
(*He has his arm.*)
I won't let you. I won't let you. That hand'll – See?
(*Lifting up his father's arm*)

MR STONE: It's no –

TONY: See? That gesture. That old gesture.

MR STONE: Tony, I can't –

TONY: You'll be just as you were. You'll be up there on that stage and your arm'll go higher and higher and higher and

they'll say, 'What a sweep! What a magnificent gesture.'
You'll lift your arm higher and higher and higher and
higher until –
(*He has been forcing his father's arm up. Finally* MR STONE
can take no more and falls forwards heavily across the bed.
SAM *and* MRS STONE *go to him.*)
GET UP, DAMN YOU! GET UP!

SAM: Why can't you let him alone?

TONY: Get off my back –

SAM: Why?

(*Fussing around the bed with* MRS STONE) I'll tidy things up,
Dad. (*Hard*) That's where it leads, all of your advice. All
your displays of love. Nowhere. They don't mean anything.
They're impotent. At least I never pretended to be anything
I wasn't. I never boasted of how perfect it all was *chez moi*.
But you and bloody Red Rosa. I mean, do you think we
don't hear things? Do you think I know nothing about your
oh so marvellous life?

TONY: What do you know about it, then?

SAM: I hear all about what she gets up to and what you get up
to. About who sleeps with who and walks out on who and
who –

TONY: Look –

SAM: Look what?

TONY: I can't explain it to you, can I? That I'm not faithful.
That she's not faithful. That we fight. That we walk out on
each other. And come back. That I sleep with men and
women and cats and dogs and people talk about what I do
and click their tongues, that sometimes I hate her, I can't
fucking stand the sight of her. But that doesn't matter,
Sam. Because I've been there. At the bottom of all that I
still love her. I love her so much I can't live without her.
I –

(SAM *is yawning elaborately.*)

I think you're trying to break me for another reason
entirely. For the same reason you worked against her from
the first time I met her.

SAM: And why might that be?

63

TONY: I think you want me to say I love you as well. That I love
you as I love her. But you and I, all of us, are so twisted
round and round each other, we can't bring ourselves to say
those ridiculously simple things. Well, I'll say it if you like,
Sam. I love you. I love you as well. And I forgive you for
what happened over Alison. And everything else. You see I
can say that. I don't find it hard to say that. I can forgive.
But can you?

SAM: It all depends how much you have to forgive, doesn't it?

TONY: You just have to forgive me for being alive, that's all.
For coming along when you thought you had all of their
love, all of their attention.

SAM: It always comes back to you being just fine and dandy,
doesn't it? And poor old Samuel having some kind of
problem that won't go away. While you seem to be living
with a woman in a ghastly parody of what love should be,
and we are expected to kneel down and worship before it.
Do you really think this act convinces anyone? Is your life
so beautiful? Is –

TONY: It's not what people do, Sammy. It's what they are. It
wasn't really Alison or Joan or Ella that came between us. It
was where we were. How we were. Somehow or other I was
able to believe in things. To look at the world and see hope
in it.

SAM: Bla bla bla faith bla bla bla socialism bla bla bla hope bla
bla bla compassion bla bla bla you really have ended up
believing your own publicity, haven't you?

TONY: These things are real, Sammy. For all I knock them.
They're real.

SAM: NOT TO ME THEY'RE NOT, SUNSHINE! TO ME THEY'RE
JUST PART OF YOUR BLOODY SMUG LITTLE SELF-
REGARDING YOUNGER BLOODY BROTHER –
(*Wild with rage he has gone over to* TONY *and is hitting him.*)

MRS STONE: SAMMY –

SAM: KEEP OUT OF IT!

MRS STONE: SAMMY!

SAM: Sammy. Sammy. Sammy. Samuel. That is my full name.
Full name, please. Can we put a statute of limitation on all

64

diminutives round here, please? I am a businessman of over
40 employing 4,000 people and in a small way doing
something for the economic life of this nation. So could
everyone in this family please stop treating me as if I were
still crawling around carrying a white rabbit and gibbering
for another cup of milk.

TONY: It was a green rabbit.

SAM: (*Really going for* TONY) SHUT UP!

MRS STONE: SAMMY!

MR STONE: Leave them . . .

SAM: 'LEAVE THEM'! (*Rounding on his* FATHER) That was always
your line, wasn't it? Leave them. But you knew she
wouldn't leave us. If she had left us I would have bloody
murdered him. But you were never real enough to matter in
any of that. You were off in some precious world of your
own, a world where I couldn't go. I was locked out of your
jokes and your shared chatter about this or that production.
I was never allowed near it. Well, I grew up to hate this
culture of yours. Because it was just another thing that
separated us, made you a remote and hopeless figure, miles
away, a voice calling faintly 'Leave them. Leave them.' The
purpose of culture to me was to make yourself look good, to
make –

MR STONE: The purpose of culture was . . .

SAM: To what?

MR STONE: To testify that –

SAM: To testify what?

MR STONE: Come here, boy.

SAM: That people grow old and die. That nobody really loves
each other. They just fool themselves they do. That in the
end you drag yourself along the floor of some public ward
and –

MR STONE: Listen. If what I did has a purpose, it would be to
show that beyond all this, beyond the mechanical, there
is . . . the thing that . . . you know . . . always . . . just
out of reach . . .

MRS STONE: You'll be all right. I'll come tomorrow anyway.
You'll pick up. I'll come tomorrow. That man at number

40 did. He had one apparently. Just what you've got. Same thing exactly. He walks and everything. I'll come tomorrow. I'll bring you a cake or something. I'll –
(SAM *has broken down.*)

SAM: (*Sobbing*) He's dying, Mum. For God's sake. He's dying. And there's nothing any of us can do about it. Nothing will pull him back. Tony's right. He wants to go. He's accepted it. That's what is so absolutely bloody terrible. He's accepted.

TONY: And maybe that's right. I don't know.

SAM: OH, DON'T TELL ME YOU'VE DECIDED TO COME TO TERMS WITH IT! DON'T TELL ME YOU'VE DECIDED TO LEARN TO LIVE WITH IT! DO YOU HAVE TO DO EVERYTHING YOUR DADDY SAYS?

TONY: Isn't this what I say to you?

SAM: WELL, NOW I'M TELLING IT TO YOU! FIGHT HIM FOR IT IF THAT'S YOUR SPECIALITY! FIGHT HIM EVERY INCH OF THE WAY, CAN'T YOU?

TONY: I can't, Sam. I've given up. I've finally given up. He's going to die. That's it. I've given up. I have to accept it.

SAM: I don't bloody accept it –

TONY: What you don't accept, Sammy, and never have done as long as I have known you is your own life. You've got so much anger but it has been allowed to grow in on itself, to block your view of everything. It's not just me you can't accept, it's all of it. Him, her, me, you . . . all of it, Sammy.

SAM: It was different when we were kids, Tony.

TONY: Yes.

SAM: When we were 3, you know?

TONY: I know.

SAM: That size. (*Pause.*) When we were small, I don't know – you'd fall over and some bigger kid would pick on you, and even though at home I was thumping you every half an hour, suddenly I'd find myself going for them, standing up for you. I was your big brother. Er . . . what I couldn't accept – you don't know how hard this is for me to say, it goes against – what I couldn't accept was that the

66

standing up for you and the thumping you – they were part of the same thing. They were . . . er . . . part of . . . part of . . .

TONY: I know. (*Pause.*) I know.

(*He goes to his* BROTHER *and puts his arms round him.*)
None of us can live without each other. Or die for that matter. We've got to hold on, Sammy, and not let them push us back and be afraid to say what we feel. There should be so much love in our family, Sam. We shouldn't allow time to do the things to it that . . . we should keep on. All of us. We shouldn't let go. None of us should ever let go.

MRS STONE: You say you don't want to be one of the little people, Tony. In the little houses. But that's all you are. All any of us are. You can't rage against that for ever. Our family is our family. That's that.

TONY: And what about mine? What about the life I chose for myself? Do you accept that? I'm asked to accept your life but do you make any effort to accept mine? Do you? Is there any chance you'll do the same for me?

MRS STONE: I –

TONY: Is there?

MRS STONE: There are things I –

TONY: She won't budge, Sam. You see her. She won't move an inch. Look at her. Granite. Solid granite, that's our mother. Go round any way you like she'll be there, waiting for you. Unstoppable. She won't move an inch. Not a fraction of an inch.

MRS STONE: I'll try, Tony. I'll try.

MR STONE: What I was saying . . . the family is . . . states of . . . conflict, again and again the same patterns . . . call the conflict 'love' or the love 'conflict' call the . . . what is necessary is the words, you know, when something's bad or good but you have to . . . you can't go round it but you have to . . . this is the word . . . you have to . . . yes . . . *accept* . . . that's the word . . . *accept* . . .

(*He falls back against the pillows.*)

MRS STONE: Sit here a bit. Both of you. Please.

(*Very slowly in their different ways they go to the bed and sit by their* MOTHER. *From the door* TERRY *comes in.*)

TERRY: Tea eaten? No tea? All a mess there. Well, well, Mrs
Stone. No harm there. All down the . . . OK there, Mr
Stone? All right there? OK? You stay. I expect the doctor
should look in. I'll have a word.

(*The family are sitting mute as he tidies round them.*)

OK there, Mr Stone? I'll be back and settle you down later.
That's the stuff. You stay there then. There we are. Were
you throwing the stuff at the wall then, were you? (*He
crosses to* MR PITTORINI.) OK there, Mr Pittorini? Put
your dukes up, Mr Pittorini. Let's be having you. Jesus,
you'll see us all off yet. (*Arranging his dressings*) Come on
there now. There's the man. Aren't you the terror of the
place yet? Aren't you a dangerous fellow now? There.
There. (*He's made the bed.*) Just beautiful. Beautiful. (*Looks
across at the family still seated on the bed*) OK then?

(*No answer.*)

OK.

(*And he goes. The family stay on the bed, unmoving.* MR
PITTORINI *thrashes once, then falls silent.* MR STONE *is
asleep. Fade the lights slowly on the figures.*)